SHOW ME HOW **BIG** IT IS!

by **Jerry Pallotta**
Illustrated by **Rob Bolster**

SCHOLASTIC INC.
New York   Toronto   London   Auckland   Sydney
Mexico City   New Delhi   Hong Kong   Buenos Aires

Thank you to Nell and Buster Douthit of
Off Campus Books, Huntsville, Alabama!
— J.P.

To Charlie, our first grandson
— R.B.

ISBN-13: 978-0-545-08583-0
ISBN-10: 0-545-08583-7

Text copyright © 2009 by Jerry Pallotta
Illustrations copyright © 2009 by Rob Bolster
All rights reserved. Published by Scholastic Inc.
SCHOLASTIC and associated logos are trademarks and/or
registered trademarks of Scholastic Inc.

12 11 10 9 8 7 6 5 4 3 2 1   9 10 11 12 13 14/0
Printed in the U.S.A.
First printing, February 2009

I'm Big!

How big are you?
Are you the biggest person
in your class?

Measure Me!

How do we measure **big**?
We can measure in height.
We can measure in width.
We can measure in weight.

Some things are just big — really big.
Large! Huge!
Humongous! Gigantic!
This man is a lineman
in the National Football League.
Wow! He is six feet ten inches tall
and three feet six inches wide!

GENERAL SHERMAN TREE

What is the biggest tree
on earth?
A giant sequoia named
General Sherman.
It is more than
forty feet wide.
People look like mice
next to it.
It's treeeeee-mendous!

General Sherman is
also very old—
two thousand years old!
That's much older
than your grandmother.

REDWOOD TREE

Or, is the biggest tree
a redwood tree?
The tallest trees are redwoods.
They grow three hundred
feet tall and can be
twelve feet wide.
They live in groves
in California.

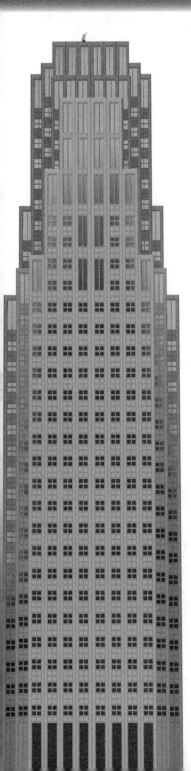

SKYSCRAPER

A very tall building is called
a skyscraper.
This building has thirty floors.
Each floor is also called a story.
The redwood and this skyscraper
are each thirty stories tall.
Someone just took
an elevator to the
skyscraper's roof.
Do you see him?

Biggest Ever!

BLUE WHALE

The largest mammal on earth
is the blue whale.
It can grow to one hundred feet long—
bigger than any dinosaur.
A blue whale can weigh one hundred fifty tons.
Its tongue weighs as much
as an entire elephant!

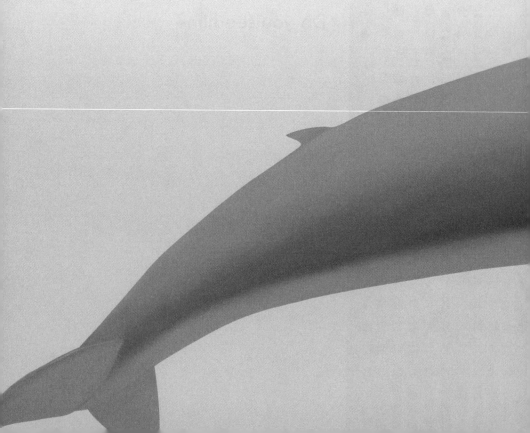

DIVER

This scuba diver is five feet tall.
The biggest blue whale is as long
as twenty scuba divers.
The scuba diver might have
a cheeseburger for lunch.
The blue whale eats four thousand pounds
of krill each day.
Krill are teeny, tiny shrimp.

What a Baby!

BABY BLUE WHALE

What is the biggest baby?
You guessed it—
a newborn blue whale.
It weighs five thousand pounds at birth.
That's two and a half tons.
It drinks two hundred fifty gallons of milk per da
Wow! That's equal to four thousand baby bottle

SNORKELER

This skin diver is swimming
with a baby blue whale.
The newborn is four times as long
as the diver.
Your mom will not let you have
this big baby as a pet!
Ask for a pet gerbil instead.

DINOSAURS

Millions of years ago,
the gigantosaurus walked on earth!
Do you hear footsteps?
Boom! Boom! Boom! Boom!
This plant eater was ninety feet long.
Some dinosaurs may have been bigger—
such as seismosaurus and argentinosaurus.

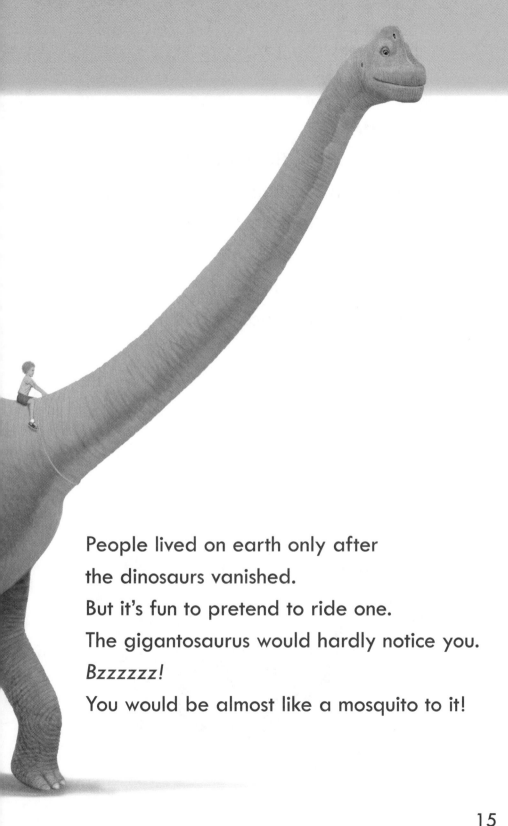

People lived on earth only after
the dinosaurs vanished.
But it's fun to pretend to ride one.
The gigantosaurus would hardly notice you.
Bzzzzzz!
You would be almost like a mosquito to it!

CAPYBARA

The capybara is the biggest rodent.
It can weigh one hundred fifty pounds.
Like other rodents, its front teeth
keep on growing.
And it keeps on gnawing.
It lives in the wetlands of South America.

BOW! WOW! RUFF! RUFF!

A capybara is bigger than most dogs.
The biggest dog is an English mastiff.
It weighs two hundred fifty pounds.
Can you take this dog for a walk?
I don't think so.
This giant dog would walk *you!*

BIGGEST COCKROACH

Speaking of BIG,
insects are the biggest group
of animals on earth.
There are millions of different species.
The biggest cockroach is from Madagascar.
It is called a hissing cockroach.
It hisses when you rub its back.
Sssssssssssss!

WALKING STICK

The longest insect is a walking stick.

It is not only long,

but also hard to see.

It looks exactly like a branch or a twig.

You can call it a stick-bug!

They can be twice as long as this book.

POLAR BEAR

Polar bears can be ten feet tall.
These mammals live
on the frozen sea.
They are great swimmers.
They are taller
than any basketball player.

ASKETBALL PLAYER

his basketball player is very big.

ut a polar bear

>wers over him.

un! Run!

bear can run faster

an a person.

olar bears love meat.

hey eat walrus, seals,

nd fish.

LOBSTER

Lobsters eat with their front four legs.
The claws can hold food
but are mostly for protection.
Some lobsters are too big for traps.
They are caught in fishing nets.

KINDERGARTNER

Kids in kindergarten have two arms
and ten fingers.
They have teeth—but they don't bite!
They have two legs and
ten toes.
You can catch them at recess.
Okay, off to first grade!

BIG, BIG, BIG CRAB!

The Japanese spider crab has legs
that are pencil thin.
Its head is small, like a football.
This crab is fourteen feet long, toe to toe.
Oops, it doesn't have toes!
It lives in the deep Pacific Ocean.

TARANTULA

The Japanese spider crab is a large crab.

What's a big spider? A tarantula!

Maybe you have one in your classroom.

A tarantula can be twelve inches long.

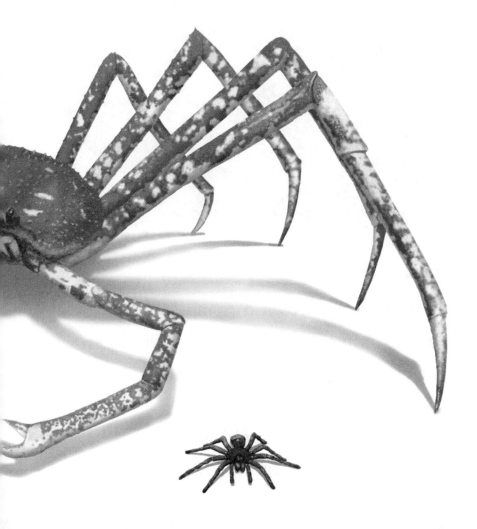

1600+lbs.

PUMPKIN

A farmer has grown a pumpkin
larger than sixteen hundred pounds.
It is huge, big, simply humongous.
When people see this giant,
they say, "Oooh! Eeeeh! Aaaaah!"
It has to be lifted by a tractor.

Another farmer decided to carve
her smaller pumpkin into a boat!
Neighbors thought she was silly.
But it worked.
Get a paddle.
Don't forget your life jacket.

JABIRU STORK

Look at this jabiru stork.

It is a huge flying bird.

It stands five feet tall

with an eight-foot wingspan.

Its foot-long beak is perfect for

catching frogs, fish, and snakes.

OSTRICH

An ostrich has it all.
It grows nine feet tall.
It is the tallest bird.
It is the widest bird.
It is the heaviest bird.
It is BIG!
The ostrich has small wings
and cannot fly.
But it has strong legs
and can sprint!

What does it mean when we say
something is the biggest?
Is it being the tallest?
Is it being the widest?
Is it being the heaviest?
"Biggest" can mean any of those things!
It depends on what is being compared
to the big thing.
That is a BIG IDEA!

Biggest Ever!

BLUE WHALE
The largest mammal on earth
is the blue whale.
It can grow to one hundred feet long—
bigger than any dinosaur.
A blue whale can weigh one hundred fifty tons.
Its tongue weighs as much
as an entire elephant!

DIVER
This scuba diver is five feet tall.
The biggest blue whale is as long
as twenty scuba divers.
The scuba diver might have
a cheeseburger for lunch.
The blue whale eats four thousand pounds
of krill each day.
Krill are teeny, tiny shrimp.

11

Glossary

rgentinosaurus: a plant-eating dinosaur that was one of the largest land animals ever

igantic: giant in size

nawing: biting or chewing with one's teeth

rove: group of trees

neman: a football player in the line, who has a specific position

umongous: very large; huge in size

odent: a kind of mammal that nibbles with its teeth

cuba: special equipment used for breathing underwater. "SCUBA" stands for self-contained underwater breathing apparatus.

eismosaurus: a plant-eating dinosaur that was one of the longest dinosaurs

equoia: the world's largest tree overall, found in California

norkeler: a person who swims at the water's surface while wearing a mask, a snorkel tube, and swim fins

pecies: a group of living things that are closely alike

anish: to disappear or go away

ingspan: the length of an animal's wings measured from tip to tip

Index

argentinosaurus 14, 31

basketball player 21
bird 28–29
blue whale 10–13

capybara 16–17

dinosaur 14–15

English mastiff 17

football player 4–5

General Sherman (tree) 6–7
giant sequoia 6–7, 31
gigantosaurus 14–15

hissing cockroach 18

insect 18–19

jabiru stork 28
Japanese spider crab 24

krill 11

lobster 22

mammal 10, 12, 16, 17, 2

ostrich 29

polar bear 20–21
pumpkin 26–27

redwood 8–9
rodent 16, 31

scuba diver 11, 31
seismosaurus 14, 31
skyscraper 9
snorkeler 13, 31

tarantula 25
trees 6–8

walking stick 19